James Aitchison

James Aitchison was born in Stirlingshire, Scotland, in 1938. He was educated at the universities of Glasgow and Strathclyde. In the 1960s he worked as a publicity copywriter at *The Scotsman* Publications in Edinburgh, after which he held a series of posts in universities in Glasgow and Edinburgh. He and his wife lived in Gloucestershire, England, for five years, returning to Stirlingshire in 2007.

James Aitchison is a former poetry reviewer at *The Scotsman* and *The Herald*. His critical studies include *The Golden Harvester: The Vision of Edwin Muir* (Aberdeen University Press 1988) and the major work of analysis and exposition, *New Guide to Poetry and Poetics* (Rodopi Editions, Amsterdam 2013). James Aitchison's textbooks include The *Cassell Guide to Written English* (Cassell 1994) and *The Cassell Dictionary of English Grammar* (Cassell 1996). He has published eight previous volumes of poetry:

Sounds Before Sleep (Chatto and Windus/The Hogarth Press 1971)
Spheres (Chatto and Windus/The Hogarth Press 1975)
Second Nature (Aberdeen University Press 1990)
Brain Scans (Scottish Cultural Press 1998)
Bird-score: twenty poems on birds (privately published 2002)
Foraging: new and selected poems (Worple Press 2009) .
The Gates of Light (Mica Press 2016).
Learning How to Sing (Mica Press 2018).

Also by James Aitchison, from Mica Press:

The Gates of Light

Learning How to Sing

Edges

James Aitchison

Edges
published in the United Kingdom in 2020

by Mica Press

c/o Leslie Bell
47 Belle Vue Road, Wivenhoe, Colchester, Essex CO7 9LD
www.micapress.co.uk | books@micapress.co.uk

ISBN 978-1-869848-27-9

Acknowledgements

Since the publication of *Learning How to Sing* (Mica Press 2018), new poems by James Aitchison have appeared in these and other journals:

Acumen, Brittle Star, The Dark Horse, The Frogmore Papers, The Herald, New Writing Scotland, Painted, spoken, Poetry Salzburg Review, Reach Poetry, The Reader, Scottish Left Review, The Scottish Review

and online in

London Grip
and
The Lyrical Aye: Richie MacCaffery
(https://richiemccafferypoetry.wordpress.com/)

No Other Animal

No other animal would scream like this –
red skin swelling around half-shut eyes,
the wet face straining back from the mouth,
the gaping mouth stretched wide around the scream –
no other animal would scream like this
unless it felt the noose around its neck
or the steel teeth grating against the bone.

The child who wants is possessed by what he wants.
He lives in the irresistible desire
of the enormous gorging Now of infancy.
Denied, the child is trapped. He cannot breathe.
Childhood becomes brute creaturehood.
Like no other animal, the creature screams
in the unfathering perfection of its rage.

The creature chokes on the scream. It gasps for breath.
It shudders in slobbering convulsions.
The head jerks up and down in terror and assent.
The child begins to breathe again.
Breached from one state of being into another,
the child falls silent, hesitant. He turns away.
His lost desire is dying in the trap.

Will

Will watched from an upper room at the Unicorn.

The dangle-dance began as a frenzied jig
and then it slowed to a swaying saraband.

Before the dangling dancer's final step
the executioner had to slash, reach in, rip out
the pulp of bowels and pulsating heart.

Walter knelt, of course, on his left knee
to receive his accolade from the perfumed queen
who was, as he had heard and still believed,
renowned for piety and gracious government.

Sir Walter knelt on both knees when he prayed
and when he waited for the headsman's axe.

Through an open window at the Unicorn
Will could smell and taste the tang
of unholy heretics' sputtering lard.

Will heard voices in the night:
the dead, the unborn and the apparitional.
He kept quill, paper and ink beside his bed
and a tallow candle burning while he slept.

Mossmen

They had no charter; they were not a guild.
Mossmen were an inbred brotherhood
who guided pilgrims across the moss -
peat bog, ten thousand acres of waterland -
to the abbey on the island in the lake.

Mossmen agreed a day, a time and a price.
They met at the bridge where paths were firm and dry.
They worked in pairs: one went ahead
and the other walked behind the pilgrims.
The leader said, 'Our spears are for water-monsters.'

The path grew narrower,
as thin as the single wavering meadow-trail
the neat-hoofed cattle made at milking time.
The trail sponged into moss;
each footprint filled with amber water-peat.

The leading mossman stopped.
He turned to face the pilgrims. 'Listen,' he said.
A water-monster is close. You hear the beast?'
His spear was angled at a pilgrim's heart.
'The danger is much greater than the price.'

'You mean a spearhead or the monster's jaws?'
'No, pilgrim. No. Our women and children starve.
Another piece of silver will save their lives.
Your crosses and your purses weigh you down.'

The pilgrims had sunk shinbone-deep in moss;
the mossmen's feet were dry. 'How can we trust - ? '
'We are the only people who know the way.
Your God cannot...' 'Our God is also yours.
We shall pray for your wives and children, and for you.'
The mossman turned his spear and offered the shaft.
'Grip with both hands and follow where I tread.'

Monsters

Sasqnatch, Yeti, Loch Ness plesiosaur -
shy creatures hide from our monstrosity.

Blackbird

When I picked up the blackbird it was dead.
It shat in my cupped hands and flew away.

Burning Books

Even when you rip the covers off
and break their spines, books don't burn readily.

Head/Blood

The first ball game was played with an enemy head.
The first red carpet was the blood of the enemy dead.

Before I Knew

With loppers, axe and pruning saw I hacked
the thickets back to less than half their width
before I knew what birds there might have been.

Filth

The name Tlazolteotl literally means, in the Aztec language, "filth goddess" ... another of her names is "eater of filth".
Neil MacGregor: A History of the World in 100 Objects

Some old gardeners swore by sewage sludge,
human excrement screened for dysentery,
an abundant crop from sewage farms.

Night soil was a family's privy waste
with added loam or ash from pruning fires.
(Fallen leaves were gathered for leaf mould.)

The filth was harvested and spread around
Roses, gooseberries and raspberry canes.
I'm not suggesting ... No. We can't go back.
At Greenyards I buy two-kilo packs
of inorganic garden chemicals -
sulphates, salts and phosphates that cost the earth.

On an Upland Moor

Nature and the man-made armatures
in these prefabricated towers
are milling invisibility, the power
of winds that blow across this upland moor.

Wind turbines are designed
to discipline wind's intermittent force
and change our course
in a land we've undermined.

Wind turbines are benign: they clear the air,
and wind's an inexhaustible free resource.

Free, but there's a price: we share a lease
with herons, curlews, swans and migrating geese.

Each turbine blade creates a turbulence
more powerful than the beating of birds' wings.
Each blade gulps air and generates intense
suction chambers in birds' thoroughfares.

When birds fly into that invisible snare
the vacuum sucks the life-breath from their lungs.

On Barra in May

I couldn't walk into the wind
made visible by flying sand.
I needed both feet on the ground
and even then I couldn't stand
upright against the wind;
I leaned on a hurricane of sound.

The west wind whummeled Barra's shore;
I tasted sea-salt on my tongue.
I stood, or stooped, for three or four
minutes with arms outstretched. I hung
my weight on that Atlantic roar
until my half-shut eyes were stung
to tears. I felt a vicious glee:
the Calmac ferry couldn't sail
in that May day's Atlantic gale.
Stormbound on Barra we were free.

In the Blink of an Eye

The Carse of Stirling will be too far south
for migrant birds from Arctic latitudes.

The Cotswolds, the Long Mynd, peaks, dales and fells
gentle lands will be intemperate.

Native birds like dippers, lapwings and wrens
will be driven north across the Pentland Firth.

Creatures that can't swim or fly
must acclimatise or die.

Supply ships', trawlers' and ferries' propeller-churn
will scramble the wavelengths and song-lines of whales.

Insects from southern Spain will settle here.
Their larvae will destroy
dog-rose, hazel, aspen, oak, beech and ash.

Changes that began in the iron age
might not last another century.
In geological time
a century is just the blink of an eye.

Edges

Corries and occluded mountainsides
immobilise your mobile phone.

Some mountains have a natural magnetism:
your compass may give false polarities.

Clouds make an all-day gloaming of the day.
You shine a torch:
the contour lines on the laminated page
don't show the edge of the precipice.

Wet rock iridesces in the sun.
Rain freezes to an invisible film of ice.

Multifaceted mountains slew the wind:
a westerly blows north, south, east and west.
You feel it fondling, groping
for a gap between your body and the rock.

Waymarks

The Ratty Burn was an ancient drainage course
that flowed so slowly the water seemed motionless
as it crossed the Carse to the Carron and the Forth.

The Ratty was just beyond the boundary
to the back garden of our new rented house.

The council enclosed the Ratty with concrete pipes
and built more homes for families from the slums.

I didn't know the rats were water voles
and their presence a proof of cleanliness.

*

A colony of black rabbits - cast off pets
gone feral? - nibbled the overshadowed grass
by the A91 just south of Bannockburn.

They were only rabbits but I learned to look out
for those black waymarks on our journeys home.

I haven't seen a roadside rabbit, black
or brown this year or last in Stirlingshire.

*

Motorway journeys were more bearable
when kestrels hovered above the verges,
eyeing the long grass for the merest twitch:
a grounded nestling, field mouse, grasshopper.

How many years of miles before I saw
kestrels hovering in their absences?

Wrens

After mild winters wrens can be as numerous as sparrows,
and yet even in good years they seem rare:
they never flock and seldom appear as a pair.

They share the same gardens as robins
but not robins' daring.
Wrens can't shake off the tic of fear.

I watch one quivering on the stone gatepost,
not cold but shivering, nerves twitching,
a frightened traveller between flights,
neither perching nor hovering on the gatepost.

It darts unwaveringly into the cover of the beech hedge.
Seconds later the hedge bursts into song.

Gooseberries

Six gooseberry bushes grown from a single plant
opened their little white five-petal flowers
in April along a south-facing sandstone wall.

The blossom weathered near-gale-force north-west winds.

I don't look for a crop in a plant's first year
but in August the branches bent with fruit.
As berries ripened, thorns grew needle-sharp.

I won't give ground to thornless gooseberries.
I need to feel the prick of harvesting:
hard barbs and soft fruit and at my fingertips.

Drystone Walls

A four-centimetre layer of soil is deep enough for grass but too shallow to hold a wooden post. And where rock beneath the soil was unbreakable, boundaries of ownership or tenancy were raised from stone.

From Cornwall to Cairngorm there are thousands of miles of drystone walls.

Hill farmers practised the Stone Age craft of masonry into the nineteenth century. Stone was harvested from however near or far: a frangible outcrop, a rock face shattered to loose stones and scree by millennia of weathering, a natural quarry by a tarn or lochan that wasn't owned by a country gentleman.

And from these sources, short thickset horses native to a place: Exmoor, Dales, Fells, Highlands, carried stones in panniers to the sites. Farm wives bore their weight in stones in wicker creels. Boys carried half-full creels of scree, stonebrash to fill hand-size crevices.

How many stones in a drystone country mile? Double that number for walls of double width.

No stone was forced into a wall. A forced stone would displace adjacent stones. Each stone was eased into its waiting place.

How did a farmer heave the heaviest stones? With wife and children as a family? In communion with men from neighbouring farms? Or were some hill farmers so hardened to the life that they developed preternatural strength?

Spirit Levels

When Stubbs of Sawtry installed a circular saw -
steam-powered, hook-fanged, inexhaustible -
the sawpit in Conington
filled up with rubble, ash and animal bones.

When Stubbs installed an electric-powered lathe
it turned more legs and spindles in a day
than any treadle-man could turn in a month.

Jack Stubbs took charge when his father, Jacob, died.
And even then hand-tools -
Stanley, tenon saws and planes -
were plied by rhythms of shoulders, arms and hands.

Stubbs' carpenters' hands were hard but their fingertips
could tell when a surface,
whatever the width of grain, was sleek enough.
And the men's eyes
were true as the bubbles in their spirit levels.

Their door-frames were scalpel-sharp as picture frames:
tremors invisible to you and me embarrassed these men.

*

There are no bridges between then and now,
no succession from these men to us.

The gaps are filled with tomorrow's yesterdays:
Samsung's and Apple's obsolescent apps.

Lose a craft and we lose a cast of mind.
Our doors are moulded in uPVC.

In Aitken's Stables

On my way to the children's library
in Hope Street almost seventy years ago
I'd stop by a window - at pavement level, barred -
of Aitken's Falkirk Brewery and look down
at the Clydesdales stabled underground.

They stood upright but with lowered heads;
Aitken's horses were sleeping on their feet.

From November to March in the early-evening dark
the dim-lit underworld outshone the street.
The sleeping horses were far away and yet -
a glint of metal from a tilted hoof -
Closer, bigger than they were by day.

There were evenings when I didn't know
I'd been kneeling until I stood up again.

At the Highland Show

Clydesdales have an inborn majesty;
handlers' white coats make them invisible.

The judge is a breeder from Nova Scotia.
He ignores the curry-comb sheen and fetlock rinse.
He looks for curvature of crest and flank,
for colouring, musculature and height in hands.
And then, a minute later, for the Clydesdale's gait.

When the judge says, 'Walk on', handler and horse
accompany each other to the edge.
They turn around and come back at a trot,
hoofbeats drumming thunder underground.

The judge knows there's no first, second or third;
there are only differences of magnificence
so slight each Clydesdale at the Highland show
could have been sired by one ancestral horse.

In a Care Home

One Sunday morning, visiting Airthrey Care,
we saw a woman brushing her mother's hair.

She wasn't just brushing;
she was stroking the crown of her mother's head.
And as she brushed she said
'Right, Mum. We'll have you looking like a queen.'

The woman plucked some white hairs from the brush
and said, 'It's silver. It's pure silver, Mum.'

The mother belched. The daughter said, 'Hush, now. Hush.'

With slow brush strokes she caressed her mother's scalp;
brushing made her loving palpable.

Stroking, caressing, the daughter brushed away
the other people in the room.

A queen? But she was talking to a child.

The mother said nothing. If she'd been struck dumb
by Alzheimer's or a stroke
what did it matter how her hair was styled?
Unless her silence was a grooming trance.

Brushing, stroking, caressing her mother's hair
the daughter made the death-house, Airthrey Care,
a place where it was safe to fall asleep.

'Another minute, Mum, and then we're done.'

Trooping a Colour

You had a mothering ferocity.
From your contempt for privilege I learned
the ignominy of the nobility.
You kept your wartime ration-book vigilance
until you lost nine decades of your life.
'Ninety-eight today? Impossible.
Take your flowers to my mother's house.'

Thirty years ago when your memory
was as clear or clearer than mine
I dreamt I was at work. I heard hoof-beats.
From my office window I saw you,
a mounted policewoman wearing a long black cape
and riding a grey horse,
patrolling a Tory enclave of Edinburgh.

Behind the back of my mind my wordless brain
invents and edits memories and dreams.
Majestic and at ease on your grey horse
you were trooping a colour I'd never seen.

The Other Queen

Huge in an open coach in summer rain
Salote, Queen of Tonga,
smiled Hello, Hello with her open mouth
and waved, waved, waved a big brown white-gloved hand.
She wore a long-stemmed flower in her hair.

Television then was the BBC,
a single channel in black and white and grey.

Rain sleeked the carriage horses:
colour-matched teams of six or four or two
were an equine hierarchy.
Queen Salote's coach was a two-in-hand
near the end of the cavalcade.

Rain blurred the closed windows
of the golden eight-horse coach of the other queen.

The day she passed through London in the rain
Salote, Polynesian matriarch,
monarch of tiny islands and coral reefs,
rejoiced in her best supporting-actress role
and in the crowd's enjoyment of her joy.

Maps of empire began to change colour that day
from imperial blood-red to tawny-green.

Four-in-hand

I heard the hoofbeats' rhythms and looked up:
from manes to fetlocks the four were black,
compact, bred for haulage, perfectly matched
Friesians of flawless lineage.

The horses were harnessed to a Victorian hearse,
a flimsy, flat-topped carriage with sides of glass.

For television? I saw no cameras.

The cortege was three stretched black limousines;
their panoramic windows were opaque.

The mourners, like the corpse, looked in the dark
and they'd be wholly insignificant
except the dead and dying keep alive
the black perfection of that four-in-hand.

Better? Or Worse?

She slots another lens into the frame
and asks me, 'Better? Or Worse? What do you think?'
Once again I say, 'They're much the same.'

'Or this?' And she inserts another lens.
I stare at the abstract pattern, stare and blink
and stare but I can see no difference.

'No? Then what do you make of this?' She tries
once more. She shines a light that magnifies
and projects a delta of pale pink
veins on a wall. Better. I see a link
from sight to visions of rivers in my eyes.

At a Stroke

'Aitchison, James: Frail, elderly, with post-stroke debility.'

Learning to Sit Still: 1

I used to say, and I behaved as if,
the purpose of a garden was gardening;
it was my seven-gardens'-long belief,
deeper here than in my previous six.

Now, at a stroke, I'm learning to sit still
or hobble along with zimmer or walking sticks:
Padded, gloved and capped against the chill
of my debility in a northern spring
I watch my small world colour-quickening
with snowdrops, crocuses, dwarf daffodils
and sparkling plum blossom, vulnerably white.

The seasons, not my horticultural skills
have the wholly earthly power to thrill me
in my eightieth as in years before.
I have reached the age - how did I reach four-score?

Learning to Sit Still: 2

Doctors say this post-stroke regimen
will last until - I don't know, don't care when.
I'll be content to harvest one last crop
of apples, gooseberries, raspberries and plums
and glean some lines of poetry like these.
I hired a gardener against my will
because my primal green belief succumbs
to my debility and age. I know I can't
be the active man I used to be.
If I had time enough, I'd like to plant
another fast-maturing dwarf fruit tree:
a Victoria plum or Conference pear
and rake out layers of moss from my horseshoe lawn.
and then, I know, I'd gladly shut up shop
having reached a stage where I don't care
as much for gardening or for poetry.
In time, the new-found cancer in my colon
or another stroke will be my last full stop.

www.ingramcontent.com/pod-product-compliance
Lightning Source LLC
Chambersburg PA
CBHW032046180726
48284CB00008B/2772
* 9 7 8 1 8 6 9 8 4 8 2 7 9 *